Tayside

The Life and Legend

Tayside

The Life and Legend

With photographs by

Douglas Corrance

Victor Allbrow   Kenneth M. Andrew   Peter Softly
P. and G. Bowater   Michael Murphy   Alex Gillespie
Harvey Wood

Commentary by Evelyn M. Hood

Collins

In collaboration with Tayside Regional Council

The Publishers wish to thank the following for their permission to reproduce photographs:

Kenneth M. Andrew 12 right, 17, 24 top, 42/3, 45, 46, 47, 56 bottom, 57 top and bottom, 104 bottom, 105 bottom, 111 top left and right, 112 top

Douglas Corrance 1, 2 bottom, 5, 29, 30 top, 31 top left, bottom left and right, 32 bottom, 34 bottom, 35, 40 top left and right, 42, 51, 52 bottom, 54 top, 58 bottom, 59-83, 84 bottom, 85-100, 101 top centre and right, 102 bottom, 105 top, 106 top, 113 top left and right, 116-17, 118 top, 119 bottom left and right, 122 bottom, 124-5, 126 top left, top right, bottom

Alex Gillespie 115 bottom

Hall Advertising Limited 15 bottom; (Victor Allbrow) 41 left, 120/21, 127; (Rod Campbell) 18 bottom right; (Peter Softly) 20 left, 23 bottom, 37, 38 top, 50 left, 107 bottom left

Michael Murphy 10, 10/11, 13 top, 44 top

Scottish Development Agency 38 bottom left and right, 39 bottom

Scottish Tourist Board (Douglas Corrance) 2 top and centre, 8, 8/9, 15 top, 16, 18 left and top right, 19, 22, 24 bottom, 25, 26 right, 27 right, 28, 30 bottom, 31 top right, 32 top, 33, 34 top, 36, 39 top right, 40 bottom, 41 bottom, 44 bottom, 49, 50 right, 52 top, 54 bottom, 58 top, 84 top, 101 top left, 102 top, 104 top, 107 top right and bottom right, 108, 109 top, 110, 112 centre, 114, 115 top, 118 bottom, 119 centre right, 122 top, 126 centre top; (Harvey Wood) 14

Tayside Regional Council 12 left, 13 bottom, 15 centre, 23 top left, 27 left, 39 top left, 41 right, 48, 53, 106 bottom, 107 top left, 109 bottom, 112 bottom, 123; (Victor Allbrow) 21, 23 right, 26 left, 55 top, 56 top, 103, 113 bottom, 119 top left and right, centre left, 121, 128; (P. and G. Bowater) 20 right, 55 bottom, 101 bottom, 111 bottom

Published by
William Collins Sons and Company Limited
First published 1983
© William Collins Sons and Company Limited
Typeset by Coats Dataprint Limited, Inverness
Printed in Great Britain by Collins Glasgow
ISBN 0 00 435675 6

Introduction

In 1975 Angus, including Dundee, most of Perthshire and part of Kinross were formed into an administrative region called Tayside — 2,900 square miles of hills and mountains, lochs and rivers, moor and lowland plain, one major city, several large towns and about 400,000 people, few of whom call themselves Taysiders.

I do, though. As an Aberdonian brought up in Fife and living in an Angus parish with a Perthshire postal address I am grateful for this means of solving any crisis of identity I might have.

For those who were born here, history goes far too deep and the sense of it is too real for a johnny-come-lately name to make its mark easily. It will be a long time, I imagine, before the people of Kinross and District will feel any real link with Tarfside on the Kincardineshire border. The old county boundaries were not simply political divisions but lines that divided different kinds of people with differing values and traditions.

One of the first things we found out when we came here in 1967 was that the old county boundary is only a field's-length away. We hadn't been here but a few hours when we learned that contrary to our supposition we were not in a between-county no-man's-land. On the evening of our moving here our very first visitor was the local bobby. He'd called to tell us a bit about our new home and our neighbours. All first-class folk — no major crime in the parish in all the years he'd been here. The only trouble he'd ever had had been with Perthshire people — thieves and poachers to a man and always had been, it seemed!

By the time he left the house the June sun had set behind the hills to the north, leaving that bright yellow glow in the sky that is a feature of summer nights here. I commented on how lovely a night it was and, taking him up on his offer of any information we might want, I asked if he'd identify for me the two hills a few fields away. I just hadn't had time to consult the Ordnance Survey map. He turned briefly to look, then said gravely, "I don't know. I said local information remember? That's Perthshire."

In the years since I have been able to discern no animosity whatever amongst the former counties. But the fact remains that the people do differ, the difference between Angus and Perthshire being particularly marked.

The reasons are doubtless historic. Perthshire was always the subject of clan feud, and people often owed their survival to the protection of clan chiefs. Government proscription notwithstanding, the clan system operated to some extent right up to the beginning of last century and even since that time Perthshire has remained very much in the hands of a few landowning families. These either have ancient titles to match their territorial claims or else came to their land by means of great trade fortunes in the Victorian era. In either case, this has meant that most of the farm land has been either tenanted or estate-run, and this seems to the outsider to have engendered in the people a certain air of deference. This may well explain why in Perthshire you find so many large and successful hotels.

In Angus, the battles for land and privilege depended less on the clan system and more on a kind of loyalty which gave a greater measure of personal independence. Here the principal fights between the Ogilvies, the Crawfords and the Lyons were over by the sixteenth century. Apart from having forever to guard their land to the west from thieving Perthshire clansmen, their faces seemed firmly turned to the sea and Europe for trade and to Edinburgh for rule. Although a lot of the land in Angus is still estate-managed, a great deal more of it is worked by farmer-owners, among whom there have been some remarkable innovators. Angus people like to think of themselves as individualists and utterly dependable. Not for nothing was the old county motto "Lippen on Angus" — rely on Angus — but this very quality can give them sometimes a seeming hardness.

The best summing-up I've ever heard of the difference between the two populations came from a retired farm worker — from Angus. "Perthshire," he declared, "has aye been a' dukes and gentry. In Angus we have lairds and fairmers. 'Deed the only thing we ever had in common was a dislike o' Dundee." Poor Dundee! I even know a lady in Fife who dreaded the opening of the Tay Road Bridge because of the easy access to Fife this would afford to Dundonians!

With a pedigree like mine I might have been expected to applaud or approve both these sentiments, but I simply fail to understand them. Dundee may not be the bonniest place in Scotland — show me a bonny industrial city anywhere — but Dundonians have a salt-of-the-earth quality that endeared them to me when I went there for my first job in the 1950s. They have a great kindness and a very quick, self-deprecating wit.

I have sadly watched most of the Dundee I first knew vanish. I have at times had my loyalty to the place tested by some of the cantrips of its City Fathers. But my real sense of attachment to Dundee has been enduring. It is my second city.

From a viewpoint of a few yards away from where I sit I can look north to Glenisla and along the Braes of Angus, south to the Sidlaws and towards Dundee, eastwards along Strathmore to Forfar, and west to Dunsinane and Perth and the Tay valley.

In image after image Douglas Corrance and the other photographers whose work is included here confirm what I have long realized — the enormous privilege it is to be a Taysider.

Evelyn M Hood

Loch Tay and the great mountains rising sheer from its water's edge are interesting evidence of great folding and faulting of the land, the making of watercourses and the scouring of Ice Age glaciers. Much later the loch became a great thoroughfare, linking the tribes of the mountainous west with the lowland population. Later still it was the route followed by the Celtic priests and learned men from Columba's west who came to evangelize the east and set up a great college at Dull on the northern shores of the loch. It was the only peaceful traffic for centuries to come, for this was the water gateway to rich pickings for marauding clansmen, and the history of warring clans in the surrounding countryside renders paltry any account of modern terrorist activity.

At the western end of the loch lies Killin, a tourist town that is unmistakably Highland. Fifteen miles east is the village of Kenmore, and although great mountains still dominate the skyline, already the land seems more lush and the trees less sparse. While the headwaters which flow into the loch at Killin must count as the true source of the river Tay, it is at Kenmore that Scotland's longest river emerges full-watered and ready for a 93-mile journey to the North Sea. Between here and its journey's end, it will sometimes meander, sometimes rush a little. Forty miles from its final meeting with the sea, estuary tides will turn the pure hill water sea-salt. Along the river's length can be traced the path of Scotland's history and much of the story of her development and trade. Romans, whaling fleets, royal regattas, salmon and pearl fishers, Viking raiders, reed cutters, great water mills — the Tay has known them all. Now, in belated recognition of its importance, its name is given to an administrative region, much of it far from the river side.

Ben Lawers, at 3984 feet, is Tayside's highest mountain and one of the highest in Britain. It rises straight up from the shores of Loch Tay, and since 1950 8,000 acres of it have been in the care of the National Trust for Scotland. The Trust's Visitor Centre and signposted nature trails have made this one of the most visited of all Tayside's high tops — and therein lies a dilemma. The plant population on the Ben is beautiful and rare. Exquisite alpine saxifrages and gentians flourish here as nowhere else in Britain and therefore must be protected.

Not only the botanists protest that to entice the nation up pathways and nature trails in a botanical paradise is to confound any serious prospect of conservation. The other side of the argument is that it is all a matter of education and control. If you tell people to keep out they only break in and do real damage. Invite them to see and to climb and to marvel for a while at the world they live in and you may well give little comfort to botanists but you will do much to open the eyes and gladden the hearts of ordinary mortals.

Botanists will recognize the pink *Silene acaulis* and leaves of *Alchemilla alpina*. Otherwise, moss campion and alpine lady's mantle.

The Cotswolds come to Campbell country? Well, not quite. When Sir Donald Currie of Garth decided to rebuild Fortingall, he ordered James Maclaren, the eminent architect, to design it in imitation of Selworthy in Devon. In the Victorian way of such matters, thus it was built, highly combustible thatched roofs and all. It is good to report that the reeds are native Scots, harvested from the Tay estuary at Errol where grows one of the largest commercial reedbeds in Britain.

Fortingall village may be Devon, but surely this is Stonehenge. Built between 1891 and 1892, Fortingall Hotel was the work of Robert Watson and William Dunn, Maclaren's successors and contemporaries of Charles Rennie Mackintosh. And in case you think "Fortingall" is misspelt, take a closer look. The second "L" is attached to the "A" in that massive lintel.

The craggy top is Meall Ghaordie, lying between Glen Lyon and Glen Lochay at the western limit of Tayside.

Glen Lyon lies to the north of and parallel to the valley of Loch Tay. The scenery varies from lush Tyrolean valley to harsh upland moor, offering a sparse living to a hardy few. The glen's history tells much of Scotland's in microcosm. Culdean monks, clan battles, croft clearances, all have had their time and place here. And now dams at the top of the glen play a vital part in the supply of hydroelectricity.

It's about six miles by Tay from Kenmore to Aberfeldy, and with that stretch of water in mind every year a marvellous mixture of men and women from all over Scotland go Huckleberry Finnicky about rafts and river currents. The unlikeliest lads get all worked up about weight dispersal and oar-thrust-to-water displacement ratios. Then in June, garage and garden-shed doors are flung wide to reveal the results of weeks of planning, sawing and painting, and at Kenmore an astonishing raft armada assembles for the Kenmore to Aberfeldy Great Charity Raft Race.

Probably it was not exactly what the Aberfeldy councillors had in mind when they bestowed on their town a Gaelic motto that translates "Fast and often rows the boat to Aberfeldy". But they wouldn't complain to see their town crammed with visitors for an event that now attracts national television coverage.

The Tay usually puts a good-humoured face on things for the day, knowing full well that not one of the rafts can reach Aberfeldy any faster than the river itself will allow.

Later military builders gave us pontoons and Bailey bridges, but in an earlier, more gracious age General George Wade sought the advice of architect William Adam and spanned the Tay thus at Aberfeldy. It stands today as a splendid memorial to Wade who, when he took command of the British Army in Scotland in 1725, saw very quickly there was no possibility of imposing the rule of law in Highland places since there were simply no roads. As with all plans for major roadworks there were objections to the scheme, not least those of the clan chiefs who had their own ideas on law and order. But Wade's military roads were built and before long had two-way traffic. Northwards the militia penetrated and subdued. Southwards the clan chiefs found high roads to the rich glens of Pall Mall and Piccadilly.

The date is carved on a large stone at Drumochter on the northernmost edge of Tayside. It marks the advance of Wade's road to this spot in that year.

Scots may argue that decorating kirk ceilings was a foreign habit we foreswore in John Knox's time. But St Mary's Church, Grandtully was rebuilt and decorated for Sir William Stewart of Grandtully in 1638, eighty years *after* the Reformation. The profusion of flowers, armorial bearings, bits of scripture and fat cherubs with trumpets are all splendidly out of key with the Covenanting times during which the work was done.

"By Loch Tummel and Loch Rannoch
and Lochaber I will go" says the song,
with scant regard for geography or
possibility. Beyond the western end of
Loch Rannoch there is a brave railway
to take you by Rannoch Moor to Fort
William. On foot you'd trek trackless
miles to find a road to anywhere. But
why move on?

In 1866 the widowed Queen Victoria
stopped here and wistfully
remembered her Highland visits with
dear Albert. More cheerfully, we've
been sharing the Queen's view of Loch
Tummel and Schiehallion ever since.

The winter face of Schiehallion is evidence that it is not simply convenience of access which brings mountaineers and explorers here to Tayside's mountains to acclimatize and train for Himalayan assaults or work in Polar regions. The scene is a far and fearsome cry from the summer-green pointed mass that is the delight of all inexpert mountain spotters. Although a mere 3,547 feet high, it is the curiously pointed Schiehallion that can be seen, recognized and NAMED from a host of Lowland vantage points. There is a shout of triumph in the name. Schiehallion! Excelsior!

Two very diverse images of the same place. The elegance of an eighteenth-century drawing room in Blair Castle and one of today's Atholl Highlanders — soldier in Britain's only private army. Together they conjure up a picture of more gracious and more troubled times when wealth and wariness were close companions.

A millwheel would make an excellent heraldic device for Tayside. At every suitable point on the course of the Tay and all her tributaries there are mills or traces of mills, spinning sheds, retting ponds for flax, and meal mills such as this. Today, much of the same water powers hydroelectric generators.

The documented history of Blair Castle begins in the thirteenth century when the central tower — Cumming's Tower — was built. Since then there has been much rebuilding and renovation according to the designs of succeeding earls and dukes. These were first Stewarts of Atholl but have been the Murrays of Atholl since 1626. Records of famous visitors here read like the *Dictionary of National Biography*. But despite its weight of history, its outer grandeur, the vast treasures within, Blair Castle remains an enchanting place where, on spring days, you may just glimpse cherubs chasing children through the grass.

In a bloody half-hour in August 1689, hope flared here at Killiecrankie of restoring the Catholic King James II to the throne, although his champion, John Graham of Claverhouse, lay dead. The hope died at Dunkeld some days later when the Protestant army broke up the Highland forces. Nothing that happened then — or since — has altered the order of the seasons nor stopped the burnishing of stones by rushing water.

Almost every parish in Tayside can boast either an existing inhabited fortress-castle or else the remains of one. In the midst of modern houses on the edge of Broughty Ferry near Dundee is Claypotts — one of the very few castles to remain unaltered since it was built for the Strachan family around 1560. Its four storeys are capped by quaint little houses which might almost serve as prototypes for the bungalows nestling below. For a time Claypotts was the home of John Graham of Claverhouse, "Bonnie Dundee", who died at Killiecrankie.

Heirs to the ancient Earldom of Wemyss bear the title of Lord Elcho from this the family stronghold, Elcho Castle. Sited on the southern banks of the Tay, four miles downriver from Perth, it is perfectly placed for surveillance of the town's river approach. And although there is nothing very homely about these stout walls, the castle might be better described as a fortified mansion with some concessions to sixteenth-century notions of mod cons. It would be some time yet, though, before gun emplacements finally gave place to curtained windows.

In 1583 James VI was only 16 when he was imprisoned here at Ruthven Castle near Perth, home of the Earls of Gowrie. There was a bungled plot to dethrone him. Later, James extracted a vicious revenge, and at their Perth house in 1600 the earl and his brother were murdered with the King's connivance. James then declared a ban on the name Ruthven both as a family and a place name. So, this is Huntingtower.

Sixteenth-century Castle Menzies at Weem near Aberfeldy has its original fortified house still in evidence despite the alterations and additions of later centuries. The ancestral home of the Menzies chiefs, it is now owned by the Menzies Clan Society which has, since 1972, undertaken the mammoth task of restoration and preservation. The best-known Menzies of recent times was Sir Robert, the Australian statesman, with deep roots in this place. Would his ancestors had been as peaceable fellows.

Built on the site of the ancient stronghold of the Thanes of Glamis. Home of the Earls of Strathmore and Kinghorne since 1372. Scene of several royal courts in the reign of James V. Pioneering place for Improvement in Scottish agriculture. Childhood home of Queen Elizabeth the Queen Mother. Birthplace of her daughter, Princess Margaret. With these few hints at a great history, and with William Shakespeare as an early public relations officer, it is small wonder Glamis is one of Scotland's most famous castles.

Set in the broad fertile plain of Strathmore, between the Braes of Angus and the Sidlaw Hills, Glamis has rarely been offstage in the drama of Scotland's history — and history was in the making here long before the thanedom of Macbeth. The area around is dotted with standing stones, ancient souterrains, mysterious sculptured stones, the ramparts of Roman encampments.

The original Glamis Castle was built in legendary times, and it seems the fairy folk had a hand in its building. It was intended to set the castle on

Hunter's Hill to the south of where it now stands. The work was begun, but each day when the builders arrived it was to find the stonework dismantled and moved to a place in the boggy valley below. Eventually, the builders gave up the argument.

Despite its often tragic history, Glamis remains an enchanting place and the most haunted of castles. Today it stands as yet another example of what happens when additions are made to an old central tower. This time the result is full of character and charm.

Centuries before this chapel was built and lavish stonework testified to pious lives, centuries before peacocks strutted on manicured lawns and guarded the Earls of Mansfield's Scottish Palace of Scone, this was the capital and sacred place to which all kings of Picts and then of Scots came for crowning. On the Moot Hill, where the chapel stands, nobles swore fealty to their king seated on the sacred Stone of Scone. From here, in 1296, Edward the Hammer carried off the Stone to Westminster. It was some time before Scottish kings were crowned on it again, and by that time they had become, and remain, monarchs of a united kingdom. Nothing remains of that early Scone, but visitors still flock here to see the Palace, its priceless treasures and its beautiful grounds.

Scone has its peacocks, Kinross House boasts lions. Inanimate, but no less guardian, they crouch on the elegant seventeenth-century balustrade, overlooking the garden and Loch Leven.

"We came upon such a lovely view — Ben-y-Ghlo straight before us — and under these high hills the River Tilt gushing and winding over stones and slates, and the hills and mountains skirted at the bottom with beautiful trees; the whole lit up by the sun; and the air so pure and fine." — Queen Victoria's *Journal*, September 12th, 1844

Pitlochry was a mere hamlet when Queen Victoria passed by in 1844. By the turn of this century it had become a popular resort for all, from the wealthy who took over entire houses for the season to the Dundee jute workers who'd pour in by train for their annual holiday on what the locals called "Tin Box Saturday". Today, Pitlochry is given over almost entirely to a thriving tourist industry, and among its chief attractions is its superb Festival Theatre where on midsummer nights can be found such stuff as dreams are made on.

Geographers say mountain rivers usually start with a downward rush and broaden to meandering waters on lowland plains. The Braan begins its twelve-mile course by wandering out of Loch Freuchie, hanging around for a time at Amulree and Dalreoch, and then takes a downward plunge, with some dramatic tumbles through Strathbraan, until it meets the Tay at Inver. Conclusion — rivers don't read geography books.

The Loch of Lowes is one of only two places in Scotland where there is a public hide for observing a pair of ospreys. The great birds put on a regular summer display of nesting and rearing young, and generally detracting attention from all but one of the many other nesting pairs in Scotland.

Had James II not abdicated, there would have been no Battle of Killiecrankie. Had Dunkeld not been destroyed in the aftermath, there would have been no such streets of Little Houses built after the fire and now restored by the National Trust for Scotland and the former Perthshire County Council. Had that care not been taken, the tourists might have gone hurrying by. Now there's something to reflect upon.

Dunkeld serves almost as a resumé of the story so far. Wade's road network forded the Tay near where Thomas Telford's bridge now spans the river. Joint capital of Pictland with Scone, Dunkeld was a place of early Christian settlement. By the time Queen Victoria paused here to marvel at the dancing of her beloved Highlanders, this was a busy market town lying on the main route between the fertile Lowlands of Strathmore and Strathearn, and Highland summer pastures. Now, probably for the first time, the town finds itself just a little way off the beaten track.

Dunkeld Cathedral took three hundred years to build and only two days to bring down. The first day came with the Reformation when, in 1560, an order went to Dunkeld from the Lords of the Congregation — "We pray you fail not pass incontinent to the Kirk of Dunkeld, and take down the hail images thereof, and bring furth to the kirkyard and burn them openly — cast down the altars and purge the kirk of all kind of monuments of idolatry."

Thus inspired, the local reformers went to work but didn't stop at altars and statues. Windows, doors and much of the roof went before the mob were brought under control and Dunkeld found itself not only thoroughly reformed but bereft of a Kirk. The second blow to the ancient structure came in 1689, after Killiecrankie, when the town was set alight. But Dunkeld folk never entirely abandoned their Kirk and continued to worship at the choir end of the old building. Thanks to Sir Donald Currie — of Fortingall fame — the choir was eventually well restored, serving as the parish church. It shelters, among others, the tomb of the notorious Wolf of Badenoch, a man who could have given lessons in cathedral destruction.

From destruction to survival. After Killiecrankie, the defeated Government army withdrew to re-form at Dunkeld. But the victorious Jacobites infiltrated the town, occupying all the houses but two — the Rectory and the Dean's House. Knowing they were outnumbered, the Government troops locked the house doors and then set the houses alight. In the morning the Jacobites were either dead or gone and Dunkeld was a smoking shell — all save the Dean's House and this, the old Rectory, which still stands close up by the Cathedral gate.

A lamb — symbol of St John and therefore of St John's Toun, Perth's medieval name, surviving now only in the name of the local football team. Highly symbolic, say the fans. Sometimes they play like saints, at others like a flock of sheep. Perth — named probably after Bertha, an old Roman camp near here on the Tay — likes to be called the Fair City. But reaction to the town depends very much on who you are. Farmers worldwide know of Perth's famous livestock markets. Habitual guests of Her Majesty link the name with one of Scotland's grimmest prisons. Tourists encounter crossroads and river-crossings and a traffic system devised by a lateral thinker. Shoppers find in Perth a cheek-by-jowl mixture of High Street chain stores, upmarket family businesses and about twenty antique shops. Australians come to look at the original. Canadians visit for the curling. Lovers of whisky come to Mecca, and old Black Watch soldiers visit the space where the Queen's Barracks used to stand. And, of course, every Scottish infant knows here is the world's smallest town — lying between two inches.

The North and South Inches are two great water meadows which were formerly islands formed by the meandering Tay. Generations of Perth folk have used them as recreation grounds. Here, on a waterlogged South Inch, St Leonard's Kirk watches a game of harbour gulls picking sides for a fight.

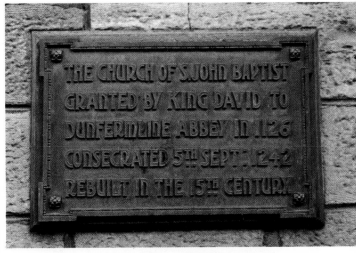

The dramatis personae in Perth's story include Agricola, every king of Scots and two Pretenders, Catherine Douglas — called Barlass for using her arm to bar a door in a vain attempt to save her king's life. Then there was John Knox whose sermon in St John's Kirk set in motion a train of destruction the remains of which we still see. Cromwell, Montrose, Wade, John Ruskin, Sir Walter Scott — and some might claim the greatest of these was Sir Walter who added another name to the list. An almost certainly fictional name, but such is the power of Scott's pen that not only do people believe that Catherine Glover, Fair Maid of Perth, lived, but believe they also know where.

Certainly the Fair Maid's House is old and glovers did live here — there were many of them in the town since it was and remains one of Perth's historic trade guilds. Perth glovers even had their own astonishing dance for very special occasions. It took the remarkable romantic mind of Scott to weave together the famous true tale of a clan battle on the North Inch with the politics of the time and a fictional tale about Simon Glover and his daughter.

As for this Fair Maid, loaded like a pack mule with the family shopping she's just managed to dash for in her office lunchbreak, where's today's Sir Walter to weave a story out of her life?

Nothing remains except names on street signs of the great Dominican monastery of Perth — Blackfriars', founded in 1231 and an early victim of Knox's cleansing. As to the Carpenters, Perth has a long-established reputation for furniture making in both local wood and in timbers brought upriver to the harbour where seagoing ships still dock.

Dominicans, Carmelites, Carthusians and Franciscans each had houses in the town — and of them no single trace remains. This former hospital, now divided into flats, stands on the site of the Carthusian monastery which was founded by James I who, not long after, was murdered at Blackfriars', a few hundred yards away. The hospital was founded when James VI — later to be another James — was only 20 years old and just coming into his own. In 1560, seven years before his birth, the old monastery had been one of the early victims of the Reformation's cleansing

Georgian terraces border both the North and the South Inch. Here, on the South Inch, in recent years some restoration has taken place. But although purists praise the face-lifting effect of pretty paintwork, they are perplexed that no one has insisted on some restoration of the Georgian windows.

The rocking horse in the window and the carved, proud horse's head serve to remind us of Perth's renown as a National Hunt racing centre with a very beautiful racecourse in the grounds of Scone Palace. The other window is in the Fair Maid's House.

In Perth, a hundred years ago or so, it seems cleanliness was the concern of the constabulary — giving a whole new meaning to that phrase "law and order".

NOTICE.

THURSDAY FIRST, 27th August, being the ANNUAL SUMMER HOLIDAY in Perth, the POLICE COMMISSIONERS have granted that day as a Holiday to the men in the CLEANSING DEPARTMENT. The Inspector of Cleansing therefore intimates that the POLICE CARTS will NOT go their usual rounds on that day, and also expects that no Rubbish or Ashes will be laid down on th Streets.

DUNCAN CUMMIN.

This, on the Salutation Hotel, must be one of the most informative of all plaques. None of your simple "Bonnie Prince Charlie Slept Here" affairs, but history with footnotes. The prince's fate we are all aware of — but how one longs to know what happened to Colonel Bower.

"Nice day to be out and about."
"Mmmm."
"Liked the blue outfit."
"Where?"
"There — to the left."
"Sorry, dear, can't look now — here's that window-dresser chap. Just hope he'll do something about this queer left hand of mine."

THE OLDEST ESTABLISHED HOTEL IN SCOTLAND (1699)
"Chambers's Journal." May 1st. 1911.
EXTRACT FROM ARTICLE "BRIDGING THE TIME — 1745-1910"
TRIAL OF COLONEL BOWER OF KINCALDRUM. FORFARSHIRE. AT YORK...
"THE ONLY CHARGE THAT COULD BE BROUGHT AGAINST HIM WAS THAT HE HAD WORN A WHITE COCKADE IN HIS BONNET, AND HAD BEEN SEEN SHAKING HANDS WITH PRINCE CHARLES EDWARD AT THE SALUTATION INN IN PERTH."
The Room Prince Charles Edward occupied is still used - Nº 20.

"Am Freiceadan Dubh" — The Black Watch. That most famous of Scottish regiments traces its origins to watch companies formed around 1725 to keep an eye on the Highlands. The tartan, which turns up both in haute couture and on shortbread tins, was of the camouflaging kind required for hill work where redcoats were, literally, a dead giveaway.

Since those earliest days, the Black Watch has seen service in every major campaign in British history. In the course of over 250 years it has earned more than 160 battle honours, among them Ticonderoga, Waterloo, Lucknow, Tel-el-Kebir, Ypres, the Somme, El Alamein, Burma, The Hook. Such history and honours make for a wealth of regimental memorabilia, and those of the Black Watch are housed in the Regimental Headquarters and Museum at Balhousie Castle in Perth.

Here are kept not only the regiment's fine silver and other ornamental treasures but the diaries and memorabilia of ordinary fighting men. Twenty-one "Watchies" have won the Victoria Cross, and their medals and records are on display. So, too, is an ensign's scrapbook of delicate watercolours and an urn of earth from the trenches of First-War France. It is a fascinating display which Black Watch Archivist James Macmillan seems prepared to defend with one of a collection of several ceremonial swords which belonged to Field Marshal Lord Wavell.

Designed in the 1820s by Adam Anderson, Rector of Perth Academy, and completed in 1832, this must have been the most elegant industrial building in Scotland. At one time it housed the steam engines that pumped Tay water from filter beds on Moncreiffe Island into the town's first piped-water system. Nowadays it is a Tourist Information Centre. No one's statue ever graced the column behind — it's the boiler chimney. But if ever Perth wants to honour Anderson, then surely there he should be. Incidentally, he also designed Perth Gasworks, but they didn't turn out nearly so bonny. Gasworks never did.

Does John Dewar the First look down on the traders below and remember how he, too, began small — a joiner from Dull who opened a wine and spirit shop in Perth High Street in 1846?

The man who owns the Bed Shop and likes to advertise large — has he ever realized that behind him stands a vast four-poster?

There was a time when the auctioneer could tell if you were bidding or not by the set of your bunnet — only townsfolk call them caps. With fewer bunnets about, his eyes have to be sharp to catch bids from fingers twitching on faces or tapping on rails, from flicked cigarettes, from barely nodding heads. New bunnets can still be seen, though, not yet broken in for casual wear. And it is still *de rigueur* to sport for luncheon what she might once have called a bonnet — even if her friends don't care that they're lowering the tone just a wee bit. Things are just not what they used to be, as she always says.

Coopering is an ancient trade that still
flourishes where there are distilleries,
since whisky is matured in oak sherry
casks. Once bottled, it simply remains
unchanged in colour and taste, but in
wood its character and "bouquet" will
subtly alter and it will age beautifully.
The men that know about such
matters usually manage to look happy
in their work.

Many of Tayside's traditional industries have had to adapt or perish in this technological age. But although it has been possible to mechanize some of the art of bagpipe making, it will be some time yet before someone comes up with a silicon chip to tune a chanter. It may be the Japanese are working on it since they are reportedly bagpipe-daft. It is to be devoutly hoped it will be some time before we hear "The Mount Fuji Reel" or "MacChoChosan's Lament".

The abundance of water to drive mills and the availability of wool and flax, and later of imported jute, for spinning and weaving, meant that for centuries more people in Tayside were thus employed than in any other industry. Fine wool cloth is still woven in centres such as Forfar, Pitlochry and Kinross. Coarse linen is made mostly in Arbroath, but from imported flax. Trials in recent years point to a revival of flax-growing in the area and the return one day of the ancient craft of weaving fine linen. For most of the jute we now find oil-based fibre, but even here there is talk of a return to natural fibre in face of inflated oil prices and diminishing supplies.

It still takes twenty-one yards of superb tartan to make a kilt, and even mass-produced jeans require skilled and deft hands to guide sewing machines. In Scotland, of course, we find it not at all odd that the breeks are for her and the skirt for him.

The area around Crieff and Perth has gained a reputation in more recent times for beautiful glassware. It isn't an ancient skill in these parts but was introduced to Perth by an immigrant Spanish glassworker between the two World Wars. Nowadays, glass-blowing, crystal-engraving and the designing of paperweights for international connoisseurs is an integral part of the Region's economy.

Hand-painting Buchan pottery at Crieff — another "imported" craft in a pottery now employing almost entirely local labour.

Barley being turned on the malthouse floor? Look again. Those are chips of pure gold being measured out at the Timex factory in Dundee, a city where a large percentage of the population is employed in the microchip industry — the golden wonder of the modern industrial world.

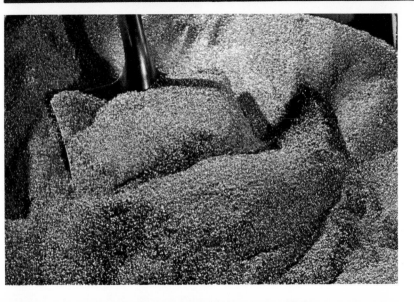

About a century ago, a certain Dr Meikle came to Crieff and built a huge hydropathic hotel on a hillside overlooking the town. The hotel is still in the family, still is a popular hotel for a family holiday, still offers special reductions to Church of Scotland ministers and their families, and, remarkable in this age, is still a temperance hotel although it is said the labels on the bottles in the dustbins would delight any oenophile. In respect of its status as a hotel without a liquor licence, Crieff Hydro appears to have a rival in the town.

In former times, miscreants were in luck if their sole punishment was to spend some time in the Crieff stocks and not be hanged from the notorious "Kind Gallows of Crieff". Judging from the crossed fingers and the slightly unsure smile, this lass knows enough local history to hope the last time these stocks were used in earnest really *was* in 1816.

Innerpeffray Library is remarkable for many reasons, not least for its setting on the banks of the River Earn five miles from Crieff and a deal more than that from anywhere else of any significance. But for almost three hundred years students and notables, ministers and ploughmen, travelled here from all over Scotland to study and to borrow books, the loan and the promise to return being solemnly entered in a volume which is now a historic work in its own right. Today you may not borrow, but you can examine and admire, amongst hundreds of other volumes, Boece's Chronicles, James VI's treatise against tobacco, and this hand-coloured copy of the Dispute of the Emperor Hadrian and the Philosopher Epictetus, printed in Switzerland in 1552.

By a wild stretch of the imagination, Comrie could be called the San Francisco of Scotland. The latter is built on the notorious San Andreas Fault line, the former on Scotland's major fault — the Highland Line. Hence they are both subject to earthquakes. But compared to Californian 'quakes, what happens in charming and peaceful Comrie is a mild shoogling — but often enough to have more recorded tremors than anywhere else in Britain.

Tremors of a different kind were probably felt in the heyday of the clan chiefs. The legend and history linked with their Highland gear can be traced at the Museum of Tartans at Comrie.

Muthill lies on the road from Crieff to Dunblane, hence on the old high road from Edinburgh and Stirling to the Highlands, and on a drove road from the central and northern mountains to the Falkirk Tryst. The tower in the long-ruined church is reckoned to date from around 1050 when there had already been an ecclesiastical centre and abbey here for around three hundred years. A latecomer to the attention of archaeologists and historians, Muthill is now designated an Outstanding Conservation Area by Scotland's Historic Buildings Council.

If St Fillan ever came back to Loch
Earn where he lived and worked a
thousand and more years ago, he'd
probably smile to see the scenery
unchanged and small boats still plying
the bonny water. But what would he
make of the folk who walk on water
and say they're only water-skiing?

Majestic Ben Vorlich and its
neighbour, Stuc-a-Chroin, dominate
the southern shores of Loch Earn. Here
the Ben, usually bright and summer
green for the tourists, wears a
forbidding winter coat.

For all its pretty views of Loch Earn and cherry blossom, Ardvorlich is a chilling place for anyone who knows the tale of a terrible thing that happened here. In 1589, a gang of MacGregors with a grudge against Stewart of Ardvorlich turned up with the severed head of the laird, new-murdered. When his sister entered the room where they were eating, it was to find her brother's head on a plate on the table, his mouth stuffed with bread and cheese. Little wonder she went mad and that her son spent his life pursuing and killing MacGregors. There is nothing new under the Mafia sun.

A kindlier, more romantic image of Scotland — the Hermitage, an eighteenth-century folly built to overlook the magnificent falls on the River Braan near Inver. It is a wonderfully dramatic place, a world away from the busy nearby A9.

Edzell Castle was the ancient home of the Crawford Lindsays of Glenesk and in its time was quite the most magnificent castle in Angus, with its large, spacious rooms and ornate ceilings. Nothing remains of the grandeur of the castle except the old stronghold tower and some walls. But, happily, we can have some idea of how beautiful it must have been since the great walled garden, laid out in 1604, still exists. This formal "pleasance", marked out by walls of the local red sandstone, was created by Sir David Lindsay, Lord Edzell, a man of great artistic sensibility who spent much of his youth travelling and studying in Europe. Represented in sculptured box and flowers are the planets, the arts, the cardinal virtues and the Lindsay family arms with their motto *Dum Spiro Spero* — "whilst I breathe I hope".

In view of that motto, we should not be surprised that it was the growing, living beauty created by Sir David which survived at Edzell long after his elegant inanimate house had crumbled away.

Another of the garden treasures that abound in Tayside, this is at Drummond Castle and was conceived on a much grander scale even than Edzell, albeit with the same notion of ordered nature. But whereas the Edzell inspiration for design was German, the Drummond Castle Garden, laid down in 1630 for John Drummond, Second Earl of Perth, is Italian in style. In the early years of the nineteenth century a great amount of Roman ornament and statuary was brought here to Italianate the theme further. And beyond the garden the eye is guided to the horizon through a woodland drive that has not a little hint of Versailles.

Unlike the old fortress-castles in the rest of Tayside, later additions to the original Drummond Castle took the form of an entirely separate mansion house alongside. This is now the Scottish home of the Earls of Ancaster, descendants of the earlier Drummonds.

It's not just Tayside castles that sprout annexes and additions and bonny gardens that need defensive walls — this time to keep back a band of marauding nettles. This house in the Carse of Gowrie is like one of those childhood toys of stacking bricks that fit neatly one inside the other. It seems to be waiting for someone to come along and put the little houses back inside the big one — and in their proper order.

A hot summer sun spotlights a beautiful sheltered corner in Aberfeldy.

Queen Victoria's *Journal* for August 31st, 1850 — "[At Coupar Angus] we got into our carriages. It was beautiful and so warm. Old Sir William Chalmers again rode with us through his little domain and wanted to make a speech, but Albert did not encourage him to do so. He took leave of us at Bridge of Callie."

Poor Sir William, laird of Glenericht just north of Blairgowrie. He'd probably spent days working up something suitable, and, beautiful warm August day or not, his new Gothic gatehouse must have looked as bleak as this as he made his way home with that speech still in his pocket.

When you tend a two-acre garden that has been described as the finest of its kind in the country, then there is every reason to look pleased with your efforts. Branklyn Garden on the lower slopes of Kinnoull Hill, Perth, is a wonderland of Alpine and Himalayan plants and was the creation of Mr and Mrs John Renton. It was gifted to the National Trust for Scotland in 1967, and gardeners flock here to marvel at such botanical delights as this *Mecanopsis* — a Himalayan poppy.

Looking equally pleased with himself is "Willie Waddell" who has, for about two hundred years, been supervising other folk's gardening. His present gardener brought him here to Mains of Dalrulzion, on the road from Perth to Braemar, some years back. He had previously wandered round Strathmore, and there is a tale that before that he had sailed the seven seas as a cabin boy. But then, when you're this old and likeable, folk will believe most things you tell them. Oh, and Willie Waddell was his name long before someone else took it and made it famous.

Mrs Bell smiles from her window in
Westfield, Blairgowrie, her window
display but a hint of the summer glory
of her garden all around you.

In Montrose, many of the older houses
are built gable-end on to the street. As
a result, one has often the delight of
finding secret sunlit gardens at the end
of dark closes.

There is a story told about Auchterarder — probably by Blackford people — that if you want to make money in the town you first open a teashop. Then when the china is sufficiently old and chipped, you change your sign to "Antiques" and sell them off. Every word of it a lie — but there are an awful lot of busy teashops and very fine antique shops in Auchterarder's long main street.

A study in symmetry —
a window in Powmill.

The famous double bridge called Rumbling Bridge spans the River Devon at a point where it plunges through a series of spectacular gorges and clefts. When the river is in spate and falls first down the Devil's Mill and then over Caldron Linn, such a roaring echoes through the bridges that they seem to rumble — hence the name. The lower was the first attempt to span the gorge in 1713. The higher crossing was built in 1816 and carries the main Crieff-Dunfermline road.

Mary Queen of Scots visited Loch Leven Castle in the spring of 1563 and spent a happy time using the fourteenth-century tower as a lodge while she and her court hunted in the surrounding hills. She even invited John Knox here for one of their famous theological sparring matches. However, the event which found Loch Leven a permanent place in Scottish history is the story of Mary's imprisonment here, and her eventual escape.

Brought here by Lords Ruthven and Lindsay as their prisoner in the summer of 1567, Mary was kept close-guarded for more than ten months. After a bleak and wretched winter suddenly there was hope of flight, and with the help of George Douglas and William Douglas she escaped the prison on May 2nd, 1568. Exactly two weeks later she was a prisoner again — this time in England from which there was to be no escape. Poor, tragic Mary.

Boats for fishermen bob at the Kinross jetty. Loch Leven boasts its own particular breed of wily fighting trout and, consequently, a whole tinful of special flies and lures just for fishing here.

Overlooking Loch Leven and Castle Island stands the classical Palladian Kinross House, built from 1685 to 1692 by Sir William Bruce of Balcaskie. By that time he'd have been well able to afford such a splendid residence, since for some time before he had been Surveyor-General for Scotland for Charles II. When the King decided to restore and extend Holyrood Palace in the 1670s, Sir William was given the responsibility for the design. The elegant façade of Kinross House greatly resembles the private apartments at Holyrood as seen from the Queen's Park.

A mile and a bit north of Abernethy, but nearer at one time, the River Earn joins the Tay. Behind the village is a hill road into Fife. Imagine, then, the need for a tower from which to overlook the rivers and the road at a time when Norsemen came a-Viking in these parts. The local Culdean monks knew precisely the fate of holy men at the hands of those particular invaders. So, in the manner of their brethren in Ireland, they built a protective tower with a doorway high off the ground. At the merest glimpse of a winged helmet, into their tower they'd run — and presumably they were right so to do since it still stands. One wonders how they chose who was to be left outside to sound the "All Clear"? In the succeeding thousand years or so, the Abernethy Round Tower has served as a place of punishment and now as a slightly incongruous clock tower.

A dugout canoe discovered near Perth a century ago is probably the oldest man-made relic in Scotland, being from 7,000 to 9,000 years old. Tayside abounds in stone evidence, too, of the people who lived and worked and worshipped here at a time before recorded history. Cairns and cists, standing stones and stone circles are to be seen all over the region. This circle stands near Kenmore.

The souterrain, or earthhouse, at Carlungie in Angus is only one of several dozen discovered in Tayside and belonging, it is thought, to the first three centuries AD. Originally, these underground, roofed stone buildings were thought to have been the houses of our Pictish ancestors, but more recent discoveries make it clear that these were the byres and silos, with the farmers living above ground nearby.

Top: from here at Ardoch near Braco in Strathearn to Stracathro at the north edge of Strathmore are the remains of strategic and marching forts set up by the Romans, led by Agricola, in an attempt to contain the native Caledonians after the Roman victory at Mons Graupius in 84 AD.

At Ardoch, one of a series of signal stations of that early campaign was overbuilt and enlarged about a century later and finally became the largest northerly outpost of the Roman Empire beyond the Antonine Wall.

History says Macbeth did *not* die here at Dunsinane (with the accent on "sin") but far to the north in Aberdeenshire. But if Shakespeare's account of events round here in the Sidlaw Hills is historically wrong, then everything he wrote of was geographically possible. There was no castle on Dunsinane but an ancient

stone and timber — later vitrified — fort on this 1,114-foot height. It overlooks the great broad sweep of Strathmore with the course of the Tay below and the Grampian Mountains to the west and north. Birnam is only a twelve-mile march across the river and the plain.

Not even Dundonians deny that architecturally much of their city is better appreciated from a distance. Empty city-centre building sites are not apt to engender much civic pride, and Dundee's city fathers for far too long adopted the maxim "When in doubt, pull it down". But despite this, Dundee folk hope you will cross the water to find out why they still think their town is special.

In simple gazetteer terms Dundee has been a royal burgh since 1190, has around 180,000 inhabitants and is Scotland's fourth largest city. It has been the administrative centre of Tayside Region since 1975.

Dundonians aren't boastful folk, but if you press them they'll tell you, in an accent all their own, about their town's long and turbulent history, of its unrivalled record in public education and the excellent health-care system in the town which boasts Ninewells Hospital, one of the most modern in Europe. Ask about famous Dundonians and they'll list you men of letters, historians, politicians, a great admiral, a soldier called "Bonnie Dundee", pioneers in flying and radio telegraphy, and the man who invented the adhesive postage stamp. For sure, the name of Mary Slessor will come up, as will Mrs Keiller of marmalade fame. But the first name you're likely to hear is that of William McGonagall, adopted Dundonian and the best of all the world's worst poets. Ask to be shown where some of these famous Dundonians lived and you'll be directed mostly to plaques and brass plates — of which more anon.

Modern bridge builders have been
likened to the men who built
cathedrals in medieval times. With
this view of the Tay Road Bridge
before us, the analogy does not seem
at all far-fetched.

Until 1966 the only road link for traffic between north Fife and Dundee was the "Fifie" — the Tay Ferry. The trip took from twenty to forty-five minutes, according to tides and sandbanks, and the boats were part of the city's folklore. Today, the journey to Fife lasts only a minute or two, with the only hindrance being a queue at the tollgates or speed restrictions in a gale — yet you still hear folk bemoan the Fifie's demise.

Between the Sidlaws and the North Fife hills the west wind can funnel down the Tay with notorious fury, driving slanting rain before it and whipping the river estuary into a white foam. Bridging the funnel is the Tay Railway Bridge, built between 1883 and 1888 to replace Thomas Bouch's original bridge, much of which was swept away on the disastrous night of December 28th, 1879. With the central section of the bridge went the 5.20 PM Burntisland to Dundee passenger train, with 75 passengers and crew on board and drawn by Wheatley Bogie Number 224.

After an enquiry during which almost all blame for the tragedy was laid at his door, Thomas Bouch became insane and died, his lasting memorial being the stumps that still remain of the piers of his bridge. The sole survivor of the tragedy was Number 224. Rescued and repaired — and nicknamed "The Diver" — the engine worked on for many years after.

Dundee's chimneys stand smokeless-zoned in unused tribute to the lum-maker's art.

Country weavers and spinners and farmers would take the City Road which leads from the once-village of Lochee to Blackness and the Hawkhill. On Sundays this was the high road to the Fifie and the braes above Newport.

Tramlines and lampposts dot the Murraygate where now not even taxis dare. The Hilltown "multis", the spire of the eighteenth-century St Andrew's Church, the Wellgate Shopping Centre in the middle distance and the foreground, that could be High Street, Anywhere — the whole makes up Dundee's accustomed jumble of not-so-ancient and compromise-modern that you find all over the city.

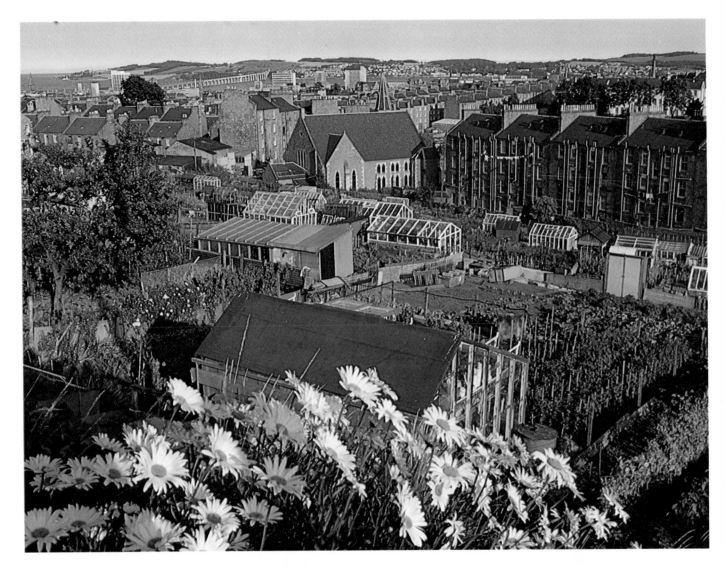

As we contemplate the neat allotments before us and ponder the Dundonian's evident fondness for gardening — there's a waiting list of 130 for the District Council's allotments alone — let us turn our thoughts for a moment to another aspect of a Dundonian which few outsiders appreciate. We mean, of course, his accent, which is so localized it ceases to exist within a few yards of the city boundary.

In the city the vowel "i", as in time, mine and high, is sounded "eh", making tehm, mehn and heh. "Ay", as in may, day and Tay, is also an "eh" sound though not laid quite so far back. Pardon, garden and market come over as perd'n, gerd'n and merkit. "T" is gulped here in the grandfather of glottal stops. Ball, law and hall are ba', la' and ha'.

With all that understood, we'd like you now to have a go at translating the following, noted down on showing a native this picture: "Eh ken whar 'at is — 'at's the gerd'ns up the La'". Turns to friend with picture, "Eh, Be'y, s'at no' the gerd'ns on the La'." Be'y shakes her head slowly, "Na, 'sno the La'. Mehnd, eh couldna seh for sure. Bit's thae no' nehs floors? Eh lehk floors, ken." Exiled Dundonians may repeat aloud.

You don't have to be very old to remember the excitement when it was Ma's day for the communal washhouse. She'd be up before light and have the fire set under the great copper boiler before you were out of your bed. Your part in the business was to help carry down the huge baskets of a week's washing and then keep out of her way for the rest of the day as she scoured and scrubbed at the big deep sinks in the sweet-sour soapy steam. At teatime, and nobody getting near the range for damp sheets and father's shirts, the last of the hot water might be scooped from the copper into the deep sinks and your littlest brothers and sisters carried to the washhouse and bathed in the soapy water. Automatic washing machines and baths with running water have rendered washdays and bathnights totally unmemorable.

In the old style of Dundee tenements you climbed through the stone tower to your front door on what in other places would be called a balcony, or a landing, or even a verandah. In Dundee this is your "plettie", or rather "ple'ie". From here you string your washing out along your line to the communal pole, or exchange banter or abuse with the folk upstairs or down. The plettie can be store room, private promenade and even stage. When it was high time for rehousing, architects soon disovered that uprooted tenement Dundonians would settle happily anywhere, provided they had either a plettie or a gerd'n.

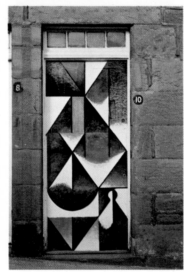

This page is assembled for the edification of the Edinburgh man who tried to tell us that Dundee was a cultural wasteland, lacking in any kind of art or elegance. Dundee has its share of classical trimmings, Doric columns and iron lace, and David Morrison's decorations are in a class of their own. Admittedly, Georgian doorways complete with flambeaux holders are a commonplace in Edinburgh's New Town, but we bet he'd never find a door quite like Number 10's anywhere else. And as for Number 53 — folk regularly take their hats off to Mr Mather's artistry. No art or elegance, indeed!

Scottish Baronial confused with French château with a dash of sultan's palace. Hollywood in its heyday could not have built a better set for some swashbuckler to burst through these doors, leap the balcony on to the saddle of a black charger and gallop away. Dundee's Central Art Gallery and Museum, this is the Albert Institute — the city's tribute to the Prince Consort, a man never once known to have buckled his swash.

A study in towering authority. The architect of the Albert Institute had an evident passion for towers — perpendicular spires, pepperpots and a heavy, mongrel style that seems to have been assembled from bits left over from the rest. Before it all sits Victoria, Queen and Empress,

immovable and probably unamused. Dundonians like jokes. This new crown for the old Queen caused cheerful traffic jams around the Institute for days.

Johnny Geddes, in the umbrella hat, has been purveying the raw material for fun most of his life. A popular entertainer and magician, his shop is a Mecca for all earnest seekers after bottomless spoons, plastic bluebottles and whirling bow ties.

Since spring 1982, Dundee Repertory Company has had a theatre worthy of the company's merit and reputation. As always, the architect had his critics, but it seems he was simply following Hamlet's advice on theatrical matters: "The purpose of playing . . . both at the first and now, was and is to hold, as 'twere, the mirror up to nature". In this case, for "nature." read Tay Square.

If it is true that "a wise scepticism is the first attribute of a good critic", here we have two good critics.

It was always a joke amongst Dundee Amateur Football League players that if you put a Hilltown team on a level pitch they ran lopsided and round in circles.

Behind these youngsters stands what used to be called the Bonnethill Church. Through that door, painted to look like a street plan, you'll find the local centre for Dundee's Inner City Neighbourhood Action Centre whose purpose, it seems, is to function as a focus for community activity as well as being a place where people can come to find friendship and seek advice. Sounds just like the old Bonnethill Church.

This is not the first blood-red hand to be seen around the old Steeple — all that remains of the fifteenth-century Church of St Mary's in the city centre. On four separate occasions this tower survived the destruction of the town around it. Hardly surprising, then, that when General Monck led Cromwell's army into the town in 1651, Dundee's Town Council moved all the town valuables here and surrendered to the General only when fires were lit at the tower base. Having first smoked them out, Monck then ordered they be killed. The Steeple survived. Local tradition always claimed that the murdered defenders had never been given proper burial, and during recent restoration work in the area their suspected remains were found — a jumble of bones in an evidently hasty grave.

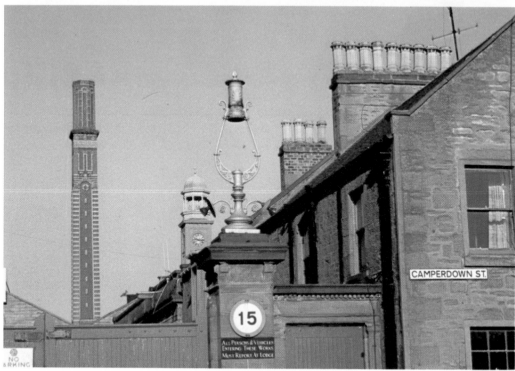

Dundee's imposing Custom House for the Port of Tay reflects the importance of its sea trade to the city. The country bus hurries on with nothing to declare.

Cox's Stack in Lochee stands over what was once the world's largest jute mill. Citizens who have watched with equanimity the demolition of much of the town they knew are moved to loud protest whenever the stack's removal is mooted. And so it stands, monument to the long ago day when there was work for all and a fortune for a very few. The street name commemorates the famous sea victory over the Dutch by Dundee's eighteenth-century Admiral Adam Duncan.

Soliloquy Number One: "Here's me, just wanting a bit of peace to ready my *Tele*, and along comes this trio of golden oldies hamming it up for a photographer. Maybe if I ignore them they'll go away. Serve them right if he puts them in his book. Daft besoms."

Soliloquy Number Two (another day in another part of City Square): "Heard it all before, but he gets so carried away he doesn't notice I'm not listening." Trouble is, nobody else seems to listen either — they just hurry on by, their ears buzzing with his megaphoned roar.

The name of the ship has a real significance for Dundee which has a large Polish community — soldiers who did not return to their native land after the Second World War, settling here to marry and raise families. Dundee has a long history, too, of trade with Baltic ports, and has a vivid folk memory of early, and often bitter, struggles to establish trade unions in the city. The door ornament of a horseshoe and the iron heel of a working boot, conveys its own story of another kind of hardworking and historic partnership.

Although warmth and shelter in the Sailors' Home are all that really matter to the seaman far from his family, we can't help wondering for how many sailors this doorway has been any kind of reminder of home.

Although younger than Nelson's *Victory*, the frigate *Unicorn*, launched in 1824, is in fact the oldest British ship still afloat, and there is hope that some day she'll be refitted with full sail. For three-quarters of a century *Unicorn* served as a Royal Naval Volunteer Reserve drill ship but now, well restored, she serves simply as a fascinating relic.

The Captain's Room in the offices of Barrie and Nairn, the shipping agent, is a salutary example to all that it is possible to run a modern business in old-world comfort. The port of Dundee once had a great number of shipping lines sailing the world in Dundee-built ships and steadily plying the sea lanes from India with loads of raw jute. Barrie and Nairn, formed from the amalgamation of two famous Dundee shipping companies, are agents still for shipping to and from Dundee and the Indian subcontinent, although nowadays the raw jute is processed mostly in the mills of India and Pakistan before being sent to Dundee.

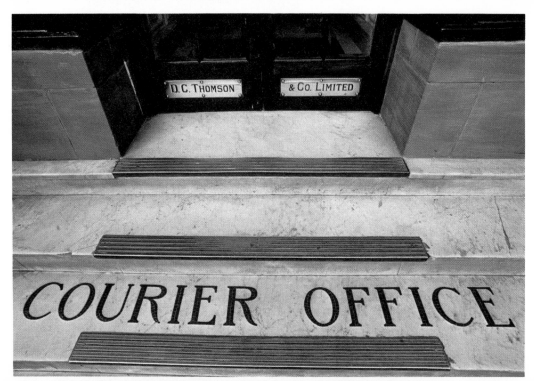

Of Dundee's three Js — jute, jam and journalism — the most durable has been the last. From two enormous city centre offices and yet another in the city's industrial estate, over 2,000 local employees of D. C. Thomson Co. Ltd annually publish and print millions of newspapers, magazines and comics.

In these offices some of the most popular of national characters have been created. Here the heroes of *The Rover*, *The Wizard* and *The Hotspur* first ran or fought their way to recognition. Here Desperate Dan ordered up his first cow pie and Dennis the Menace and his dog Gnasher first set off to harry poor Walter, while the mayhem of the Bash Street Kids probably broke out on another quiet desk a few feet away. All that is created here has that particular quality of humour that leaps generation gaps and leads grown men to hide their *Beano* in their *Playboy* centrefold.

But for Scots at home and abroad there is a set of cartoon characters without whose adventures in *The Sunday Post*, the sabbath would be a sad affair. These are, of course, The Broons who live at Number 10 Glebe Street, and Oor Wullie, with his dungarees, tackety boots, tousled hair and upturned bucket. All were the creation of the brilliant cartoonist Dudley D. Watkins, who, we remember, looked a bit like Wullie's arch-enemy P. C. Murdoch. Watkins convinced us all that, jings and crivvens, we have met folk just like these, although nobody we know has remained unchanged for nearly fifty years. Wullie has, in recent years, been transferred successfully to the stage. We cannot think why the same hasn't happened to The Broons, having long visualized Phil McCall as Paw.

The Weekly News, begun in 1855, was printed in local editions in its early days, hence "The Dundee" on the old advertisement. Today there is only one edition which sells throughout the country. *The Courier and Advertiser* is a daily paper serving Fife, Tayside and Kincardine, and is almost the last newspaper in the country to devote its front page exclusively to advertisements. *The Evening Telegraph* — Dundee's "Tele" long before the birth of John Logie Baird — is the city's evening paper and is here apparently determined to uphold its critics' claim that it headlines too much trivia.

Dealing in trivia is an accusation often levelled at the company whose answer is, as always, to ignore the accusation and just go profitably on. The Thomson family is also accused of being paternalistic, introverted, and secretive about sales and financial affairs. There are those who say the Registered Office plates are set at the foot of this door because the company thinks outsiders would do better to approach the premises with reverence — and preferably on their knees. But even the critics do not deny the company's tremendous success, the loyalty of its staff, its enviable pension scheme, and its training policy which has fitted generations of young journalists for editorial desks the world over.

Even if she was born an Aberdonian, Dundee has always claimed Mary Slessor as its very own earthly saint. It provided the gruelling training of coping with a drunken father, hard mill-work and grinding tenement poverty, coupled with the comfort she found in her Christian faith, that fitted her for her life's work as a missionary in Nigeria. Mary Slessor lived and worked there from 1876 to 1915 and is still remembered and honoured in that country. Dundee's particular memorial to a remarkable woman takes the form of these two stained-glass windows in the City Museum where there is a collection of objects and photographs telling the story of her life.

Dundee walls are stippled with plaques of the "On This Site" variety, but this potted biography stands under a cherry tree in a shopping mall, and we often see visiting Canadians reading it — which is as it should be. They paid for it.

A long history of wine trading in Dundee and along the east coast explains grapes as an inn sign on an old wall in Hilltown.

A study of Dundee's ancient burgh court records shows that justice was often tempered with mercy — that is, unless you were a woman who either committed adultery or hurled abuse at your neighbours. Then you might find yourself being led about the town in one of these branks, a target for physical abuse. And in the same headgear, through which you could neither eat nor drink, you might be attached by a chain to the town wall while your feet were clamped in stocks. For men, this punishment seems to have been reserved for cheats and thieves. Feminists will have fun finding reasons for these medieval inequalities.

"See's fehv pehs."

"Pehs — no brehdies the day?"

"Nuh! Eh think a peh's a bra' denner."

"Brehdie's is good an' a' — ingin een's onywye."

"Eh prefer them plehn — no ingin."

"Meh!"

"Here, eh'm in a hurry — see's thae fehv pehs."

We looked along the shelves of pipe tobacco jars and saw Uncle Tom's Mixture, the Black Isle Mix, Sailor's Pride. Tin number 2 with Dundee Mixture was self-explanatory, but number 8, the Toffee Mixture, had us puzzled. Did the tobacconist sell sweeties as a sideline? Oh no! Toffee Mixture is a caramel-flavoured tobacco — Dundee's tobacco equivalent of prawn-cocktail crisps.

The Hilltown was for many a century a separate barony within Dundee, and the main thoroughfare still rises steep behind the Wellgate. Much of the Hilltown, like Dundee's other hilly satellites, Hawkhill, Blackness and Lochee, has vanished in recent years in the name of progress, the briefly exposed braes again vanishing under new factory developments or housing schemes. Much of the Hilltown is given over to multistorey blocks where even on the ground floor you can have a fabulous view south over the Tay to Fife. The old post office has, so far, eluded the planners' attention.

Raise your eyes above his carry-out to that beautiful window and see if you can spot the camera. In 1889 this was the photographic studio of W. Lowden and Son who first make their appearance in the Dundee Directory in 1858 as "Artists and Photographers" in Elizabeth Street, making them amongst the first, if not *the* first, commercial photographers in the city. We suppose the Lowdens will have to wait till their building is demolished before they get their plaque.

The Morgan Tower in the Perth Road is part of the Morgan Buildings, built in 1790 and designed by local architect Samuel Bell. He it was who designed St Andrew's Church at the other end of the town, the windows here being typical of his style. Would that the same attention to window style had filtered down to the latterday designers of the ground floor shop — but here we are again with Dundee's mix of nearly old and partly new.

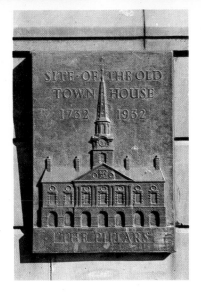

For two hundred years William Adam's Dundee Town House — affectionately and always known as The Pillars — stood in the space that is now City Square. In 1932, this building and the historic town houses that lay between it and the river were swept aside to make way for the vast Caird Hall and the new Council Chambers, in what was a staggering example of planned vandalism, even by Dundee standards. Certainly, Dundee needed both the hall and new chambers — but not at such a cost to civic pride, still regretted and resented by Dundee folk.

Some pubs survive in spite of slow service, but at the top bar you'll wait forever. It stands in Dundee Museum and is a mixture of the interiors of the Old Toll Bar, Lochee, and the John o' Groats in the Cowgate, rescued when the buildings around them were demolished. So here stands a silent pub — more eloquent tribute than any plaque to generations of earnest quenchers of mill and factory drouth and the hardy, friendly folk who pulled the pints and poured the nips.

Happily, not all has been lost to the bulldozer or the cocktail and carpet trade. In the Speedwell Bar nothing much except the prices has changed in nearly a hundred years. Even electronic games are tucked away in corners for fear of interference in the proper function of a good pub.

Dundee and Dundee United are Scottish Premier Division football clubs, each with an avid following. In another place, the rivalry could be deadly, but in Dundee interclub fan warfare is practically unknown despite the two home grounds being so close together the floodlights of one could easily illuminate the other. And it is not unusual to find, for instance, Dundee supporters — club colours concealed — cheering on United in Cup or European matches; a courtesy returned by United fans when it's Dundee's turn to play.

Opposite and top left, young United fans are seen practising queueing at Tannadice for their future seats and being kind to the underprivileged — in this case a stray St Johnstoun supporter from Perth, here for a Tayside Derby. Opposite and top right, it is obvious that the juveniles referred to in the notice in the lower left picture have found their own way of interpreting the law even if, as a Member of the Association, you could end up behind bars.

Meanwhile, at Dundee's ground, Dens Park, the whole of the agony and ecstasy of ninety minutes is caught in a split second.

The Dundee mixture as everywhere —
low rise and high rise, villa and
tenement, church spire and factory
stack, threatened old and tarnished
new.

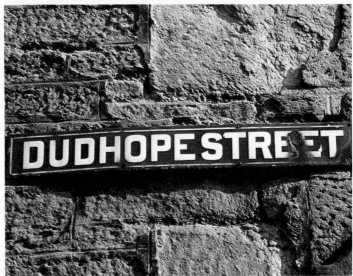

About nine feet of harled wall separate the top left and top right notices. Perhaps the Council had learned its lesson after the fun that's been poked in the press and on television at the notices in Paradise Road. But only strangers to the town find any drear significance in Dudhope Street. Dudop, it's pronounced, and it's named after a castle in the town.

Roofs and chimneys and three rooms in
search of a view. While, not far away, a
publishing house that was once the
city's Assembly Room and Coffee House
contemplates its own reflection in a
windowed walkway in the Regional
Council headquarters.

If we have seemed at all disparaging over Dundee's efforts at modernization and redevelopment, the time has come to redress the balance a little and compliment the planners on one important facet of their city centre plans — the provision of seats around flower beds, on cobbled patios, under trees. So popular are these seats that on any summer's day, and even on wintry Saturdays, people can be seen queuing up for a place on a bench. What a pleasure they are, and what a chance to rest a while, share your dreams, your opinions and even your lunch with a friend or a passing pigeon.

Some more attempts by us to impress
the Edinburgh critic. Dundee, too, has a
West End.

The Magdalen Green lies between the Tay Railway Bridge and the Perth Road. It was in nearby Step Row that William McGonagall lived. When he wrote his tribute to the rebuilt bridge, the Magdalen Green was a gift of a rhyme to the frantic poet.

"From North, South, East and West,
Because as a railway bridge thou art
 the best,
Thou standest unequalled to be seen
Nearby Dundee and the bonnie
 Magdalen Green."

Luckily for Dundee, there have been later and greater artists to record the Green — most notably the landscape artist J. McIntosh Patrick whose home overlooks the Green and who has painted the scene in several memorable pictures.

For all the size and sprawl of Dundee, no one in the city lives more than a few minutes from either the countryside or the shore of the Tay. In addition, the city boasts almost 1,500 acres of public park, the largest being Camperdown, gifted to the city by descendants of Admiral Duncan. Dundonians seem sometimes overwhelmed by the size of the park and sit huddled together in comforting groups. Only the uninhibited children and the selfabsorbed musicians make free with the air and space — but woe betide them if they drop a scrap of paper or even a note.

It was suggested to us, by the way, th. the grouping on the park bench indicates an element of racial prejudi *Not* in Dundee where, because of its 150-year-old link with the Indian subcontinent, people have been long accustomed to welcoming Asians into their midst. Indeed, they are so much part of the Dundee scene and commercial life that an Asian family now owns Keiller's famous sweet factory — and things don't come more Dundonian than that.

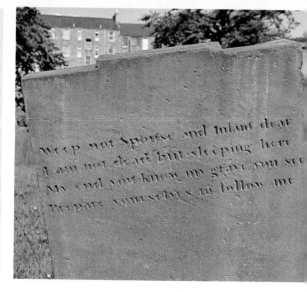

Some notices are easily understood, such as the one on the wholesaler's window which makes it quite clear that wine comes before whisky on the east coast of Scotland. Some, as in the tiled close, make it subtly clear that here is the entrance to no ordinary tenement but to one as "wally" as any in Glasgow.

Some are a puzzle — until our resident medical student pointed out that the knee is a unique mechanism. (Forgive us if we still suspect people refer to 152 Perth Road as "that old joint".) As for the Lochee gravestone – whenever and however did the author spell it out and set it down?

What strangers have to understand
about Dundonians is that even when
they tell you that distance lends
enchantment to a view of their town,
they are not seeking your agreement on
the matter. It is therefore in the hope
we shall not be misunderstood that we
say we think this shows that Dundee
can be both enchanting and beautiful,
even if it is in the near dark with the
light behind it.

In summer, the *Tay Queen* sails upriver from Broughty Ferry to Perth and back — a pleasure cruise, a geography lesson and, for the older generation, an exciting chance to recall how the old Fifies used to cross at just about here.

On the skyline behind the slipway is Broughty Castle, a defensive tower that used to guard the approach to Dundee and is now converted into Dundee's Whaling Museum.

For almost 150 years whaling was a major activity based on Dundee, and last century it was the presence of the already well-established whaling industry that assured the development of the town's jute industry. Originally, successful processing of jute depended upon this special lubrication.

Dundee was not only famous for its whaling captains and men, but also for its home-built fleet of sturdy whalers, the most renowned of which was the *Terra Nova*, Robert Falcon Scott's choice for his last Antarctic expedition.

A study in sunbathing styles at
Broughty beach, with one person at
least succeeding in staying in the sun
and avoiding it at the same time.
Meanwhile, man burns and dog learns
the true meaning of "dog days".

Coupar Angus is an ancient place where once there was a great Cistercian abbey of which nothing now remains but a few stones in the corner of the churchyard. According to the inscription on the side of this tower, this is the "Tolbooth Steeple built by public subscription in 1762. Prison of the Court of Regality" — a reminder of even earlier times when justice in the name of the king was meted out by his representative on the spot, the town's Superior.

The escutcheoned gateway, complete with bishop's crozier, leads into the church that stands where the Abbey once did. Beyond the boundary wall, and as far as the eye can see, is the broad rich farmland of Strathmore.

There are few days in the year when Blairgowrie folk have their town to themselves. In summer the area throngs with berry-pickers from every corner of the globe, for this is the heart of the largest concentration of soft-fruit production in Europe. Tourist buses share the town's streets with tractors hauling loads of rasps and strawberries, and Mr Irvine and his colleagues are kept hard at it victualling the army of pickers.

The summer season of work and play ends on the first Saturday in September in the Wellmeadow where townsfolk, visitors and the returning hordes from the Braemar Gathering meet up, in splendid festivity.

The Ericht, tributary of the Isla, flows through the twin towns of Blairgowrie and Rattray, and the salmon run on the river, when the big fish come up to spawn, is a remarkable scene. Not a few parr, mistaken for minnows, end their days prematurely circumnavigating local goldfish bowls.

The beech hedge planted in 1746 on the Marquis of Lansdowne's Grandtully estate at Meikleour has the distinction of being the world's highest hedge, presenting, therefore, the world's biggest headache for hedge trimmers. A majestic sight all the year round, the hedge is particularly lovely when the new leaf comes on in the spring and when the mid-autumn sun catches the glowing golds and browns.

Long before the berries, spinning and weaving were Blairgowrie district's most important industries, and old and abandoned mills lie all along the Ericht, once their source of power. The first raw jute brought to Scotland was spun here in a Blairgowrie mill belonging to the Grimond family. Blairgowrie, with its jute and berries for jam, could once have laid claim to two of Dundee's famous Js.

On summer days, sunny or not, in Strathmore and on the Carse of Gowrie the race goes on to bring in the tender fruit. Pickers are paid by the punnet or weight. A premium is often paid for selective picking for canning and freezing — less for buckets of berries for jam. An expert picker can make good money, particularly when she brings her own family squad along to lend a hand — and who wouldn't be happy with a chance to nibble at perks like these?

Yellow fields of oilseed rape have
become a common sight in Tayside in
recent years. Working farmers in the
Region have a particularly fine
reputation for enterprise and a
willingness not only to experiment but
to apply their skills to improving
techniques of crop husbandry. Oilseed
rape is amongst the most recent in their
list of successes.

Hill lambs have to be tough to survive
— but *this* tough?

Old farmworkers have fond memories of bothy days when the pecking order from orraloon to grieve was adhered to as strictly as any regimental protocol. A man knew his place, a lad learned by watching his elders and superiors and working alongside them at the ploughing, the sowing, hoeing, and harvesting. And at the end of the day, with the horses cleaned and fed and settled for the night, there would be music to make with the fiddle, the melodeon and the "moothie". There was a camaraderie bonded in toil and sweat that the modern tractorman, earmuffed and alone in his warm cab, knows little of. The work is still hard but does not rack. There are few companions. All of which is why old men and young visit the Folk Museum in Glamis Village and equally marvel at how things have changed.

Fat cattle take their éase in fields above Lundie in the Sidlaws, ruminating, perhaps, on the fact that they are considered amongst the best-cared for cattle in the country thanks to another breed you find round here — the cattlemen.

Scotland's seed potato trade is concentrated almost entirely on the east coast and particularly in Angus. Here, near Brechin, backs bend to bring in the crop, for, in spite of developments in mechanical handling, there is still much work for tattie squads. The importance of potatoes to the rural economy is such here that schoolchildren in Angus are allowed a two-week break in October so that the older scholars can help with the harvest if they want to — whereas, in other parts of the Region, schools close for one week only.

At a Game Fair near Crieff we looked at this silent group for some time before it dawned on us that they were all trying to remember on which calendar it was they'd last met up.

Nowadays the Clydesdale horse in Scotland is rarely kept for work but is rather breeding stock to supply American brewers with picturesque dray horses. The old harness-decorating tradition is still maintained, though, and such is the real bond between horse and horseman that we are certain we're interrupting here a three-way conversation.

The blackface is a remarkable sheep, offering two layers of fleece for use in making strong tweeds and carpets and, curiously, for stuffing mattresses in Italy. In addition to fathering lamb chops and supplying the wherewithal for sheep's head broth, the sheep knows just how to win admiring glances at rural shows when, in a final sacrifice, he gives up the raw material for the ancient and beautiful craft of turning crooks and walking canes.

Two factors link the archers with the steam engine. The first is that both events take place in the grounds of Glamis Castle, and the second is that the bows and arrows and steam engines we all flock to watch were once — and in their day — a commonplace.

Aficionados — there is no equivalent word in our language — of Highland Games flock where the best heavyweights turn out to compete. Each of these "greats" has his own technique, his own individual approach to the matter of chucking around lumps of iron or flipping over cabers, both of which go hard on high hopes and singlets. In former times, heavyweight competitors had also to prove themselves as runners and dancers, and the collection of shoes round the competitor's feet may well include still a set of spikes and a pair of delicate dancing shoes — although the latter we doubt.

Noblesse oblige — even when it means obligatory attendance at the Dunkeld Highland Games in proper country rig in the full blaze of a summer's afternoon.

Much more fun and comfort, we suspect, is the shirt-sleeved order and the cool of the beer tent watching someone else sweat it out at sheepdog trials at Aberfeldy.

The red deer has only one natural enemy in Scotland — man. Man, got up in special stout tweeds and waterproofs, will belly-crawl for days through autumn heather in pursuit of stags, which probably accounts for the superior expression on most stags' faces, even when they find themselves stuffed or, worse, bodyless and nailed to inscribed bits of wood.

Until 1982 the Seventh Duke of Atholl, telescope at the ready, looked down on this splendid "Royal" stag. Today, this corner of the entrance hall at Blair Castle is occupied by a portrait of the Tenth Duke depicted with a more modest trophy at his feet — a pair of dead wood pigeons shot in defence of growing crops.

We are taught that keeping to the straight and narrow is a difficult thing — duly rewarded. Who'd have thought it also makes one impervious to bullets.

Our first thought about the stalkers' railway, above left, that ran from Dalmunzie Hotel, near the Devil's Elbow, two miles west and up to Glen Lochsie Lodge was that this was just the kind of solution to a transport problem our Victorian ancestors blithely undertook. We then learned to our surprise that this line was not laid until the 1920s and for no very practical reason except that the man who ordered it built did so because his brother had done the same thing in the Ayrshire hills. Hauled by a Simplex two-cylinder twenty-horsepower petrol engine, a train of two flats and two seated carriages climbed from 1,200 to 1,700 feet in two miles along a twenty-seven-inch-gauge track. The little train made its last run here in 1979 to uplift its tracks. Engine, track and train are now at the National Tractor and Farm Museum near Hexham in Northumberland.

Amazing numbers of fishing rods and flies are bought in Britain each year, fuelling a long-held suspicion of ours that the equipment is meant to catch anglers not fish. But, in Tayside, the theory is confounded. Here there are so many famous fishing rivers, fed by so many burns, that fish there are aplenty for the taking — provided you have the right skills, patience and, on certain stretches of water, a healthy bank account. But even if you have none of these, there are some fine opportunities to catch a bit of quiet, some calm and a little restoration of the soul beside still, deep-running water.

In Tayside Region's guide to hill walkers, suggested climbs are graded A, B and C. Grade A marks easy climbs for family outings. C is for the experienced and fit. In winter, this ridge on Meall nan Tarmachan to the north of Loch Tay by our reckoning rates around Z.

Not for the first time in these pages do we want to set a picture to music rather than words. Hum "The Campbells Are Coming" to this — and you'll see what we mean.

From the solitude of the winter hills to the roarin' game, as polished granite scuds the ice at a bonspiel near Blairgowrie.

Bob Hope said, "If you watch a game, it's fun. If you play it, it's recreation. If you work at it, it's golf!" Tayside abounds in first-class links and some of the country's finest inland "workshops" — where sometimes, as above at Gleneagles, things go wonderfully right. Isn't he going to wish he'd watched, because she's certain to analyse that stroke forever.

The "umbrella" is at Carnoustie whence came a host of great professionals to found the sport in the United States.

Peter Pan piping down the Glengate to one of Kirriemuir's old kirks reflects both J. M. Barrie's best-loved fictional creation and the "kailyard" books he wrote about Kirrie's fighting weavers and their penchant for religious dispute.

Sir James Matthew Barrie, a weaver's son, was born in this white house on the Brechin Road, Kirriemuir, in 1860 and was buried in the town's graveyard in 1937. He is a revered figure in his native town where pilgrims come from all over the world to visit his birthplace, the little washhouse which was his first theatre and the historic town he called Thrums. Few writers have succeeded as Barrie did in imposing a character as well as a name on a town — and still be loved. But natives foster the image of a douce, quaint Kirriemuir, preferring to be known for its Barrie rather than it Ball.

Nestling in the Braes of Angus, foothills of the Grampians, are some of the most beautiful glens in all Scotland. Not dramatic stony clefts in mountains but gentle river tracks, glacier-cut through time-smoothed hills and backed by the steep-rising Grampians. Glenisla, Glen Prosen, Glen Clova, Glen Doll, Glen Lethnot, Glen Esk — each has a distinctive character all its own. Here, in Glen Clova, cattle graze in the warmth of the summer sun and an old world stands still. It is difficult to imagine that it was to these particular glens that Robert Falcon Scott and Edward Wilson came to train and plan for that last tragic expedition to the South Pole. But glen weather up on the tops in winter can be severe, fast-changing and treacherous.

Sixty years ago in an Angus school, a wee lad from a large family was asked what he'd want if a fairy godmother granted him one wish. His answer — "a haill Forfar bridie tae masel'."

Nobody knows exactly how the bridie originated — it bears a striking resemblance in shape and content to a *chausson d'Auvergne* — but this king of meat pies continues to engender lively debate and rivalry amongst baking establishments in the town.

In its long history Forfar has been the scene of other battles. An ancient seat of Scottish kings and an important religious centre, its parish church stands on the site of a Celtic chapel.

Nearby, at Restenneth, are the ruins of one of Scotland's oldest churches close to where in A.D. 710 St Boniface baptised Nechtan, King of the Picts. The medieval spire sits atop a building which may be the church Nechtan buil here.

116

Brechin Cathedral was begun in its present form in the early years of the thirteenth century, replacing a Norman church which had, in its time, replaced Celtic buildings. The round tower belongs to the Celtic time, like the one at Abernethy, except that this managed eventually to get itself attached to the later building, be capped with a little spire all of its own, and be more ornate and all-of-a-piece than its contemporary. Its purpose was probably identical, though, being a place for hiding holy men and holier relics from prowling, sticky-fingered Vikings.

The City and Royal Burgh of Brechin owes much of its history and its early development to its ecclesiastical importance, and street names still reflect that past — Maison Dieu Lane, Chanonry Wynd, Bishop's Close. Latterday Brechin is a weaving and engineering town and a market centre for Strathmore to the southwest and the Howe of the Mearns to the northeast. Until the town was blessedly bypassed, the main Perth-Aberdeen route included the streets of Brechin where about one heavy lorry a week failed to take one or other corner, and the populace were noted for their nimble, traffic-dodging footwork. Even yet, it seems, a few still await the challenge of a moving car or two.

In the graveyard of Portmoak Church lies Michael Bruce, a weaver's son born in 1748. A classic lad o' pairts, he died of consumption at the age of 21 while studying for the ministry at Edinburgh University. According to local lore, the Reverend John Logan, a university friend, undertook to publish Bruce's poems posthumously and a slim volume of his works did eventually appear, but Bruce's family complained immediately that Michael's so-called Gospel Sonnets had been left out of the book. The story goes that Logan said they'd been accidentally burned. These sonnets were rhymed paraphrases of Bible passages which, some years later, Bruce's family claimed, were published under Logan's name. Many of the paraphrases are still sung in church. Michael Bruce has a cottage museum and an annual church service to his memory. The Reverend Logan appears to be forgotten — except around Portmoak.

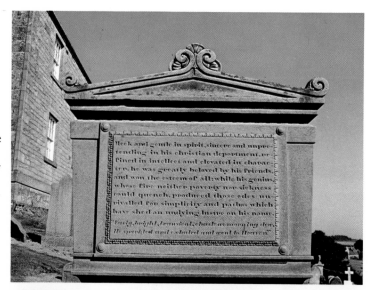

When James Faichney, master mason, planned and carved his family memorial stone to be set in the Innerpeffray Chapel graveyard at the end of the seventeenth century, he included on it not only the traditional symbols of mortality and the dates of birth of his ten children but also statuettes of them all. Boys are shown in kilts or the short-skirted coats of the time, the girls in long dresses, and all are ranged according to their ages. His parents, placed on either side, bearing fruity confections on their heads, flank Mr and Mrs Faichney. The severe face above may well be a depiction of a stern Divinity, or perhaps it is Mr Faichney's mother-in-law. Perhaps one model served for both.

Awesome, mute testimony of the Dark Ages. No one is yet certain why the Picts sculptured great stones and slabs. Are some of them pictorial accounts of actual events? Are they simply the tombstones of chiefs and heroes whose names are forever lost to us? What precisely do they signify, those recurring symbols of mirrors and dragon heads and the intricate interlacing? In the east of the Region a large number of these stones are to be seen. Some are outdoors, like the three great stones shown here from Aberlemno. Others, such as the famous collection of twenty-five from Meigle, are kept protected from weathering in their own museum in the village.

The little stone rests against the north wall of the ancient graveyard at Innerpeffray Chapel — and marks burial layers at this point. The position of other layers are indicated by carvings at the base of the chapel wall, but this historic burial place has long been closed for want of room.

In churchyards all over Scotland old stones are decked with symbols of death, man's mortality and the certainty of final judgement. But on some stones, as on the right, care is taken to make certain that even the illiterate get the message. Here lies a tailor, symbolized by the tools of his trade. Other common signs are ploughshares and yokes for farmers, shuttles and looms for weavers, combs and distaffs for spinners, spades and rakes for gardeners.

Looking across from Arbroath harbour to the Signal Tower which is now the Town Museum, people who don't know Arbroath might be forgiven for thinking that's all there is to the place — fish and history — but they'd be wrong. Engineering and weaving have long been of far greater importance to Arbroath, which has a population of around 30,000. The Signal Tower gets its name from being just that — a means of signalling from atop their shore base to the men who manned the famous Bell Rock Lighthouse, twelve miles out at sea.

But even if the day came when there was nothing left to Arbroath except its fish, it would still know better how to deal with a haddock than does any other place on earth. The Arbroath Smokie is a culinary masterpiece, and the art of making it was brought into the town by fisherfolk from the cliff village of Auchmithie, just to the north. Oak chips are set to burn at the bottom of a buried barrel or lined pit, then smoored to smoke under a heavy cover. The fish are gutted and hung in matched pairs on racks. These are then suspended under the cover and over the smoke for half an hour or so. The method is easy to convey, the result defies description.

The great Abbey of Aberbrothock was founded by William the Lion in 1176 and dedicated to St Thomas à Becket. For centuries, a lamp was lit in the great "O" of the south transept window as a guide to seamen. From time to time, a great pageant is staged in the Abbey ruins, which tells the story of the writing here of a letter from the nobles of Scotland to Pope John XXII, petitioning him to recognize their leader, Robert the Bruce, as their rightful king. The claim was acknowledged. The letter became known as Scotland's Declaration of Independence, but the Abbey fell into ruin and faded out of history. It has made one brief reappearance. In 1951 the Stone of Scone was brought here some time after having been removed from under the Coronation Chair in Westminster Abbey. For a day or two Scots were reminded, if they ever knew, of the part Arbroath's Abbey had once played in the country's story.

At the "fit o' the toon" the younger men of Arbroath line up for what will doubtless one day be their place in the scheme of things.

Three miles of red sandstone cliffs and stacks and deep inlets lie between the old fishing village of Auchmithie and Arbroath. Auchmithie is the Musselcrag of Scott's *The Antiquary*, but even Scott could not have composed better than the local names for some of the natural features on this coast — Needle's E'e, De'il's Heid, The Pint Stoup, The Crusie, the Mermaid's Kirk. This last lump of cliff bears an uncanny resemblance to Snoopy.

Ask five people at random in Montrose old High Street what is the most important feature of their town and you'll get five different answers. Its position on a spit of land with the North Sea on one side and the Montrose Basin on the other. Its long history as a trading port and the international trade it still does from its busy harbour. Its beautiful streets of classical buildings constructed either with merchant money or as seaside homes for Angus lairds. Then there's its history — the links with the illfated Marquis of this Ilk and the town's involvement in the Jacobite rebellions. Someone is sure to tell you the story of how, more recently, with about £4,000 in funds, the Harbour Board took courage and asked central government for a loan of about £4,000,000 to build a supply base for oil rigs. They got the loan, built the base and have repaid the money in record time. If all of this isn't enough for you to take in at a time, then move on to the next five you meet and they'll talk of the salmon fishing industry based in the town. Someone is sure to mention the Petroleum Industries Training Board school. You might hear about the town's fame once as a centre for silversmiths and as a place of education. Perhaps you'll hear how the Montrose folk themselves get their name "Gable-endies" from the habit the old landowners had of building their town houses gable-end to the High Street, allowing not only privacy but quiet garden space. But there is one thing the folk you talk to won't tell you and that is that their town is the finest in Angus. They expect you to know that without being told.

A bell called Big Peter sounds curfew over Montrose every night at ten o'clock. Generations of bellringers have climbed the steeple to ring the bell and whiled away the spare minutes decorating the wooden walls of the bell room. Unwittingly they have created a piece of history every bit as valuable as the tower around. Conservationists, please note.

Warm lights glow in a Montrose antique-shop window. The sun finds its way into one of the hidden gardens that surprise the eye at the end of entrance closes.

Two at least of Montrose's closes have literary connections. On their famous Scottish tour in 1773, Boswell and Johnson lodged at the Ship Inn in the close off 107 High Street. Johnson was impressed by the town's neatness. Boswell reported in his *Journal* that they visited the town hall, admired the Episcopal church, thought the gable-end-to-the-street houses looked "awkward". When, as Boswell reports, he had to remind Johnson "that episcopals were but dissenters here; they were only tolerated. 'Sir,' said he, 'we are here, as Christians in Turkey.'" Almost 150 years later a young man some thought of as a literary Turk among Christians came to Montrose to work on a local newspaper. Chris Grieve was the name he went by here; Hugh MacDiarmid is his name for posterity.

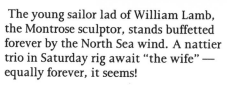

The young sailor lad of William Lamb, the Montrose sculptor, stands buffetted forever by the North Sea wind. A nattier trio in Saturday rig await "the wife" — equally forever, it seems!

The Montrose Basin is a great tidal
lagoon, and only when it drains at low
tide can the River South Esk be seen
meandering through to the sea. At one
time the river mouth divided in two,
looping round Rossie Island to meet
again with the harbour on the north
shore and the old fishing village at the
south. In the North Sea oil — supply —
base construction plan we've already
mentioned, the harbour extension was
achieved by blocking the southern river
mouth. The few objectors to the scheme
quickly accepted the worth of the plan
and Ferryden found itself landlocked.
But the Basin and its mussel beds and
reed beds remain unchanged, and
naturalists flock here to study migrant
birds drawn by the twin pleasures of
protection and good food.

Daytime and nicht,
Sun, wind and rain,
The lang cauld licht
O' the spring months again;

The braird's a' weed
And the fairm's a' still —
Wha'll sow the seed
I' the field by the lirk o' the hill?

Violet Jacob

128